Exercise for Physical & Mental Health

An Integrated Life of Fitness

Core Workouts

Cross-Training

Eating Right & Additional Supplements for Fitness

Endurance & Cardio Training

Exercise for Physical & Mental Health

Flexibility & Agility

Sports & Fitness

Step Aerobics & Aerobic Dance

Weightlifting & Strength Building

Yoga & Pilates

An Integrated
Life of Fitness

Exercise for Physical & Mental Health

Z.B. HILL

Mason Crest

Mason Crest
450 Parkway Drive, Suite D
Broomall, PA 19008
www.masoncrest.com

Printed and bound in the United States of America.

First printing
9 8 7 6 5 4 3 2 1

Series ISBN: 978-1-4222-3156-2
Hardcover ISBN: 978-1-4222-3161-6
Paperback ISBN: 978-1-4222-3199-9
ebook ISBN: 978-1-4222-8699-9

Cataloging-in-Publication Data on file with the Library of Congress.

CONTENTS

Introduction   6

1. Exercise and the Body   9

2. Exercise and the Mind   27

3. Exercise and Your Future   35

4. Making a Plan for
   Physical and Mental Health   45

Find Out More   59

Series Glossary of Key Terms   60

Index   62

About the Author and the Consultant
   & Picture Credits   64

KEY ICONS TO LOOK FOR:

Text-Dependent Questions: These questions send the reader back to the text for more careful attention to the evidence presented there.

Words to Understand: These words with their easy-to-understand definitions will increase the reader's understanding of the text, while building vocabulary skills.

Series Glossary of Key Terms: This back-of-the book glossary contains terminology used throughout this series. Words found here increase the reader's ability to read and comprehend higher-level books and articles in this field.

Research Projects: Readers are pointed toward areas of further inquiry connected to each chapter. Suggestions are provided for projects that encourage deeper research and analysis.

Sidebars: This boxed material within the main text allows readers to build knowledge, gain insights, explore possibilities, and broaden their perspectives by weaving together additional information to provide realistic and holistic perspectives.

INTRODUCTION

Choosing fitness as a priority in your life is one of the smartest decisions you can make! This series of books will give you the tools you need to understand how your decisions about eating, sleeping, and physical activity can affect your health now and in the future.

And speaking of the future: YOU are the future of our world. We who are older are depending on you to build something wonderful— and we, as lifelong advocates of good nutrition and physical activity, want the best for you throughout your whole life.

Our hope in these books is to support and guide you to instill healthy behaviors beginning today. You are in a unique position to adopt healthy habits that will guide you toward better health right now and avoid health-related problems as an adult.

You have the power of choice today. We recognize that it's a very busy world filled with overwhelming choices that sometimes get in the way of you making wise decisions when choosing food or in being active. But no previous training or skills are needed to put this material into practice right away.

We want you to have fun and build your confidence as you read these books. Your self-esteem will increase. LEARN, EXPLORE, and DISCOVER, using the books as your very own personal guide. A tremendous amount of research over the past thirty years has proven that the quality of your health and life will depend on the decisions you make today that affect your body, mind, and inner self.

You are an individual, liking different foods, doing different things, having different interests, and growing up in different families. But you are not alone as you face these vital decisions in your life. Those of us in the fitness professions are working hard to get healthier foods into your schools; to make sure you have an opportunity to be physically active on a regular basis; to ensure that walking and biking are encouraged in your communities; and to build communities where healthy, affordable foods can be purchased close to home. We're doing all we can to support you. We've got your back!

Moving step by step to healthier eating habits and increasing physical activity requires change. Change happens in small steps, so be patient with yourself. Change takes time. But get started *now*.

Lead an "action-packed" life! Your whole body will thank you by becoming stronger and healthier. You can look and do your best. You'll feel good. You'll have more energy. You'll reap the benefits of smart lifestyle choices for a healthier future so you can achieve what's important to you.

Choose to become the best you can be!

—Diana H. Hart, President
National Association for Health and Fitness

Words to Understand

motivation: Your reason for doing something.

endurance: The ability to exercise for a long time.

tissue: A certain kind of material inside our bodies that do one kind of job. Tissues are made up of just one kind of cell.

contract: Shrink or get smaller.

dilate: When something circular gets wider. For example, your pupils and blood vessels dilate when they get bigger.

stroke: When a person has a blood clot or is bleeding inside his brain.

capacity: The greatest limit of something's ability to do something.

thermostat: Something that controls the temperature.

Chapter One

EXERCISE
AND THE BODY

People exercise for all sorts of reasons. They exercise because they think it's fun. They exercise because they want to look a certain way. Some people exercise because they like to compete. Others exercise because they like the emotional rush it gives them.

But whatever our *motivation* for moving our bodies, exercise changes us. It not only changes the way we look on the outside, but it also changes the way our internal organs function. It changes the way our hearts and lungs, kidneys and intestines work. It even changes the way our very cells do their jobs.

Our bodies are built to move. They're designed to meet challenges. The more we exercise, the stronger we become. If we haven't been

Starting a new exercise plan can be tough, but fighting through a few tough workouts will be worth it in the end.

Exercise for Physical & Mental Health

Make Connections

Researchers think that for every minute you exercise, you could add on 7 to 8 minutes to your life!

exercising regularly before, the changes won't happen all at once when we start an exercise program. It takes time. And it's not easy—especially at first, when our bodies aren't used to working so hard.

When you start an exercise program, the first thing you'll notice is that you are breathing harder than usual. You may be able to feel your heart pounding inside your chest. Everything in your body is connected; each part works together with all the other parts. So as your muscles start moving more, your heart and lungs work hard to do their jobs as well, so that your muscles will have what they need.

Here's what's happening. Every cell in your body needs oxygen in order to function. Your muscle cells are no different. When your muscles work harder, they need more oxygen. Your lungs suck in oxygen from the air, working faster and harder than normal. Your blood picks up the oxygen from your lungs and carries it to your heart. Then your heart pumps extra hard to get the oxygen-filled blood out to all the cells in your body, especially your muscles' cells.

If you're not in very good shape and you start exercising, at first, you won't feel very good. Your heart, lungs, and muscles aren't used to all the extra work. But if you keep at it, after a few days, you'll notice some changes. You'll be able to do the same exercise without breathing as hard. Suddenly it seems easier. That's because your muscles have changed. They're using oxygen more efficiently now. Your lungs and heart don't have to work so hard to get extra oxygen to your muscles.

Make Connections

Even though damaging your muscle tissues can be a good thing, you don't want to injure your muscles in ways that could keep you from being able to continue your exercise program. A pulled muscle is something totally different from the kind of tissue damage that makes you stronger. A muscle that's been torn or strained can be extremely painful. Mild to moderate muscle pain is normal and healthy—but extreme, severe pain isn't. So start slow. Don't push your muscles too hard at first. Build up gradually. Give yourself days off in between strenuous exercise or work on different muscle groups on alternate days. Always make sure to stretch and warm up before any strenuous exercise.

HOW EXERCISE CHANGES YOUR MUSCLES

Depending on what kind of exercise you're doing, your muscles could change in a couple of different ways. The muscles in your arms and legs have two kinds of muscle: fast-twitch muscles and slow-twitch muscles. Fast-twitch muscles are what help you perform short burst of activity, while slow-twitch are good for *endurance* exercise over a longer period of time. When you start an exercise program, you probably have about the same amount of both kinds of muscles. But if you start a plan that involves exercises like swimming, bicycling, or jogging, you'll soon build up more slow-twitch muscles. This means that your muscles will be able to keep working for a longer period of time without getting tired. They won't put the same oxygen demands on your heart and lungs. The opposite would happen if you focused your exercise program on something like weight lifting, where you needed your muscles to put out short bursts of power: you'd soon start to build up more fast-twitch muscles. Your muscles change, depending on the demands put upon them.

Make Connections

When a healthy heart pumps at full force, about 20 to 25 liters of blood flow through it every minute. So imagine what a liter-sized bottle of soda looks like—and then picture 25 of them. That's how much blood your heart can pump in just one minute when you're exercising!

No matter what kind of muscles you're building, when you first start any sort of new exercise program, your muscles will probably feel pretty sore. That's because exercise actually damages your muscle cells at the microscopic level—and that damage hurts! But it's actually a good thing. When muscle *tissue* is damaged, it responds by repairing itself. The repaired tissue is actually stronger than it was before. And don't worry—the soreness won't last forever! After a day or two, your muscles will start to feel better.

No matter what kind of exercise you're doing, your muscles are working together to make you move. That's the whole point of exercise. Whether it's big movements or small, your muscles are working to pull your bones and move your entire body. As they do so, they put demands on the rest of your body.

When you exercise, your muscles are a little like the motor inside a car. Like a motor, your muscles use an energy source to generate force. A car's motor burns gasoline for its fuel; your muscles use a chemical called adenosine triphosphate (ATP).

When your muscles move your body, they *contract* and release, like rubber bands pulling your bones. ATP is needed for the chemical reactions that take place whenever your muscles contract. As the muscle works harder, more and more ATP gets used.

As your muscles "burn" ATP, they need three things:

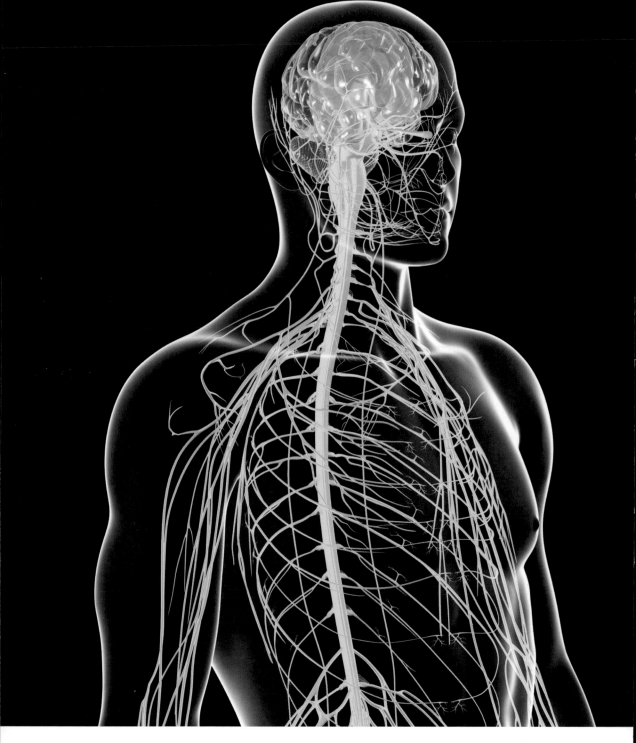

The nervous system controls your body's movement, sending messages from your brain and spinal cord to your muscles.

Exercise for Physical & Mental Health

Make Connections

None of the changes that take place in your body when you exercise could happen without messages being carried through the nervous system. Your autonomic nervous system—your spinal cord, brainstem, and all the nerves that do their jobs without any conscious thought on your part—jumps into action every time you exercise. The nerves carry the messages to your heart, lungs, blood vessels, and all your other body organs, telling them what to do to get more blood to your muscles.

- oxygen to produce the ATP.
- a way to get rid of the waste, the way a car's exhaust pipe gets rid of the waste products left over when gasoline is burned; when ATP is "burned," the waste products are carbon dioxide and lactic acid. (Lactic acid is what makes your muscles hurt. When it builds up in the muscle tissue, it causes some of the soreness you feel after exercising.)
- a way to get rid of heat, similar to the way that a car's motor needs coolant to keep it from getting too hot; working muscles generate heat in the same way that the moving parts of a car's engine also generate heat.

A car needs a steady stream of fuel flowing into its engine for its motor to keep working—and your muscles need to keep making ATP in order to keep moving. To make this happen, your body must supply oxygen to the muscles and get rid of the waste products and heat. The more strenuously you exercise, the more help your muscles will need from the rest of your body. If your muscles don't get what they need, you won't be able to keep moving. You'll get exhausted, and eventually, you'll have to quit.

Whenever you lift a weight, many different systems in your body work together to allow you to flex your muscles and raise the weight.

Exercise for Physical & Mental Health

Make Connections

When you are sitting down, you only take in about 15 breaths a minute, giving you around 12 liters (almost 13 quarts) of air every minute. From this, your lungs will get just one-fifth of a liter (not quite a cup) of oxygen. During exercise, though, athletes may increase their breathing rates to around 40 to 60 breaths a minute. This means they take in 100 to 150 liters (about 105 to 160 quarts) of air, extracting around five liters (a little more than 5 quarts) of oxygen every single minute.

So whenever you exercise, your body parts all work together to give the muscles what they need. Each time you exercise, your entire body—all the organs and systems, from your heart to your skin, from your circulatory system to your nervous system—gets busy doing whatever it needs to do to help your muscles do their job. Your body is pretty amazing!

HOW EXERCISE CHANGES YOUR HEART, BLOOD, AND BLOOD VESSELS

Your heart is actually a muscle—so some of the same things that happen in your leg and arm muscles when you exercise also happen in your heart. If you work out regularly, your heart muscle will get stronger and bigger. This means it won't have to work so hard to push your blood around your body. When you're exercising, the amount of blood flowing through your heart increases by about four or five times. Because the muscle is more powerful now, it doesn't have to move so many times to do the same job. This means your heart rate will slow down, both when you're resting and when you're exercising.

At the same time, exercise is also good for your blood vessels. As you exercise, the blood vessels in your muscles *dilate*. To understand

Smoking will keep you from being in the best shape you can be, making it hard to breathe while exercising and preventing you from exercising as long as you could if you didn't smoke.

Exercise for Physical & Mental Health

Make Connections

You need healthy lungs in order to exercise. Smoking will affect your ability to exercise. If you quit smoking, though, you'll notice the difference pretty quickly. In fact, you're likely to be able to exercise longer and more easily as soon as two weeks after your last cigarette.

how this helps your muscles get more blood, imagine the difference between using a garden hose and fireman's hose; the bigger the hose, the more water can flow through it. The same thing happens with your blood vessels—as they get larger, more blood can flow through them to your muscle cells. When this happens every time you exercise, it's like a workout for blood vessels. They become more elastic, so you're less likely to have a *stroke*. Your blood pressure will be lower. All that makes your entire body healthier.

Your circulatory system (your heart, blood, and blood vessels working together) does all this to help your muscles have what they need to exercise. Whenever your muscles move for more than a few minutes, they need a fresh supply of oxygen. If they don't get it, they won't be able to keep moving. So your heart and blood work together to get extra oxygen to your muscles whenever they're moving—and then your muscles cells pull the oxygen out of the blood. A muscle that's working is able to get three times the amount of oxygen from the blood as the same muscle can when it's just sitting there, not doing anything. Meanwhile, your circulatory system is also sending less blood to the body organs you don't use as much while you're exercising—and sending that blood instead to your working muscles. With everything that's going on in your body working together, your muscles will be getting almost fifteen times more oxygen when they exercise than they do when you're sitting on your sofa watching television.

Exercising regularly will improve your lungs' ability to get oxygen to your muscles, allowing you to work out for longer periods of time.

Exercise for Physical & Mental Health

Evaporation of sweat removes fluid from the body, so you'll need to drink extra water when you exercise to maintain the fluids your body needs for blood flow and sweat production. Sports drinks can also replace minerals like sodium and potassium that are lost in the sweat, and they provide additional glucose for energy. Without enough fluids, your body can't cool itself down. This could cause heat stroke, which is a very dangerous condition.

Your body makes sure that plenty of oxygen-rich blood flows to your muscles. Now your muscles need to get the oxygen out of the blood. This is where the red blood cells in your blood come into the process. A protein called hemoglobin, in your red blood cells, carries most of the oxygen in the blood. Hemoglobin can attach itself to both oxygen and carbon dioxide molecules. It picks up oxygen from the lungs and carries it to the muscles. Then, in the muscles, it picks up carbon dioxide, which is a waste product your muscle cells create. The hemoglobin in your blood carries the carbon dioxide back to your lungs, where the carbon dioxide is released as you exhale. Then you inhale fresh oxygen—and the whole cycle repeats. As more blood flows to your muscles, the cycle happens faster than usual. This makes you breathe faster too.

HOW EXERCISE CHANGES YOUR LUNGS

While your nervous system is getting the message to your circulatory system to respond to your muscles' needs, it is always sending messages to your lungs. These messages will increase the rate and depth of your lungs' breathing. At the same time, as your heart beats harder, your blood pressure increases. If you think about a water hose again, increased water pressure inside the hose means that more water flows

Make Connections

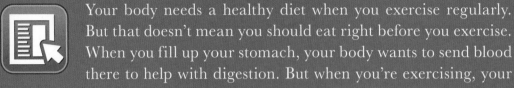

Your body needs a healthy diet when you exercise regularly. But that doesn't mean you should eat right before you exercise. When you fill up your stomach, your body wants to send blood there to help with digestion. But when you're exercising, your blood needs to go to your muscles. If you eat a big meal right before you exercise strenuously, you make a conflict inside your body. You may end up with a stomachache—or muscle cramps. It's better to eat a couple hours before you plan to exercise.

through it faster—and the same things happens inside your blood vessels when your blood pressure increases. This increased pressure inside your lungs pushes open more tiny air sacs (alveoli), allowing your lungs to work at their full *capacity*. Imagine trying to fill a water balloon with a hose that doesn't have much water pressure—and now picture how much easier it would be to inflate the balloon with more water pressure. You could think of each of the little air sacs in your lungs as being a little like a water balloon. With all those little air sacs expanding as big as possible, you can suck in more oxygen from the air.

When you exercise, your nerves also send messages to the muscles that help you breathe—your diaphragm and the muscles between your ribs. The messages tell these muscles to tighten and relax more often, allowing you to take more breaths. And like all the other muscles in your body, the more often you give them a workout, the stronger they get, and the more you're able to handle strenuous exercise.

HOW EXERCISE CHANGES YOUR SKIN

As muscles "burn fuel," they produce heat, just like the engine of a car does. This is why you get hot when you exercise. Your skin is the part of your body that helps you deal with all this extra heat. Your skin will

Your immune system is made up of the parts of your body that help you fight off germs and other invaders that could make you get sick. Recent studies have shown that people who exercise at least a few times a week get far fewer colds than people who don't. Scientists have found that exercise gives a boost to the cells in your body that fight disease. These cells apparently work more slowly when people don't exercise—and they speed up for a few hours each time people exercise. Too much exercise—exercising longer and harder than your body is used to doing—can put a strain on your immune system, however, and make you more likely to get sick. It's important to build up slowly to a regular, lifelong habit of exercise.

feel hotter to the touch, you'll get sweaty, and you may look flushed. All these are signs that your body is working hard to cool you down.

The heat produced by exercising muscle makes the blood vessels in your skin dilate, which allows more blood to flow to the skin. This is what makes your skin feel hot to the touch, and it's also what may make your skin look flushed when you exercise. The blood carries heat in it, but when it reaches the skin, that heat can escape into the air around you.

The nerve cells in your body also carry a message about the excess heat to your body's *thermostat*, the hypothalamus in the brain. The hypothalamus sends out nerve messages that tell the skin's sweat glands to produce sweat. The fluid for the sweat also comes from the increased skin blood flow. (Remember, all the body's systems work together!) The sweat evaporates from the skin, removing heat and cooling the body.

Research Project

The sidebar in this chapter on page 19 indicates that smoking can make it harder to exercise. Use the Internet and the library to find out more about how smoking affects your body's ability to exercise. Does it slow down or weaken any other body systems necessary for exercise? Write up your findings. Include diagrams or images that show the difference between a nonsmoker's organs and a smoker's.

HOW EXERCISE CHANGES YOUR DIGESTIVE SYSTEM

To make ATP, your muscles also use glucose. Glucose is a form of sugar. Your cells get energy from the process of breaking glucose down into carbon dioxide and water. The glucose can come from a few places:

- supplies in the muscles
- from the liver, which sends the glucose to the muscles through the blood
- absorption of glucose from food in the intestine, which also gets to your muscles through the bloodstream
- from your body's stored fat

Even when you're not doing anything, your body needs energy for all the things that are constantly going on inside your body, things like breathing, blood flow, and growing and repairing cells. We use calories as the unit of measurement for talking about the energy we get from food and drinks. Your digestive processes change the calories you take in when you eat and drink into energy your body can use. It's a very complicated chemical process, called metabolism, which combines the calories with oxygen to release energy. When you exercise, your metabolism speeds up, and you burn even more calories. When you burn more calories than you're taking in, your body will start tapping into the places where it stores up energy—your fat cells. This is why exercise can help you lose weight. It gets rid of your body's stores of fat.

A MORE EFFICIENT BODY

Exercise brings changes to your entire body—and these changes are good for you. They help your body work at its greatest possible capacity. They make you healthier, better able to resist diseases and heal after injuries. You'll be able to handle all the unexpected demands life sends your way (like running to catch a bus—or running to get away from a bad guy). You're likely to live longer. Exercise affects every system in your body. Even your brain!

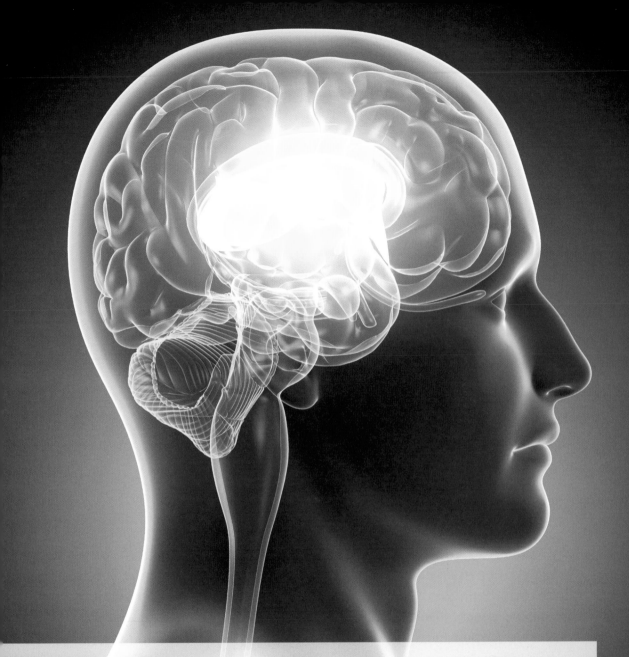

Words to Understand

anxiety: When you feel worried about something.
neuroscientists: Scientists who study the brain and the nervous system.
researchers: Scientists who find the answers to questions and make new discoveries.

Chapter Two

Exercise and the Mind

Your brain is a part of your body. Sometimes people seem to forget that. They talk about "mind and body," as though they were two different things. Actually, though, your brain is a vital part of all the systems that make your body function. It's a little like the command center for everything that goes on inside your body. Without your brain and nervous system, the rest of your body wouldn't be able to do much at all. And just like exercise helps the rest of your body, it also helps your brain work better. In fact, exercise not only makes you

Getting active will relax your mind and improve your mood, no matter what kind of workout, sport, or activity you try.

28   Exercise for Physical & Mental Health

healthier, but scientists think it also may make you both happier and more intelligent.

EXERCISE AND EMOTIONS

Your emotions—the feelings you experience in response to the world around you—are actually chemical reactions taking place in your brain. Happiness and sadness, fear and anger, and every other emotion you have are all caused by chemical changes within the nerve cells—the neurons—inside your brain.

Several different brain chemicals help to produce your emotions. Endorphins are chemicals that help you cope with pain; they also make you feel happy. Adrenaline helps your body get ready for danger, so it's connected to your feelings of fear and *anxiety*. When your brain releases dopamine, it gives you a burst of pleasure. Serotonin, yet another brain chemical, plays a role in your feelings of happiness and sadness, as well as your feelings of both grouchiness and peace.

Exercise, researchers have discovered, makes your brain release its chemicals in ways that make you feel better emotionally. Strenuous exercise—the kind that makes your heart and lungs work harder—can

Make Connections

When you breathe, your brain uses about one-quarter of all the oxygen you take in.

Exercise can help reduce stress by releasing chemicals in your brain that help you calm down and lessen anxiety.

Exercising just a little bit can have great effects on your mood, but exercising regularly is one of the best ways to get your mind in shape along with your body.

make your brain may send out a burst of endorphins that give you a "high." But the good feelings don't end there. Regular exercise can help regulate your moods, so that you feel calmer and happier all the time. Strenuous exercise also reduces the amount of adrenaline in your body. This means you can handle stress better. You won't feel as anxious or nervous.

Exercise and the Mind   31

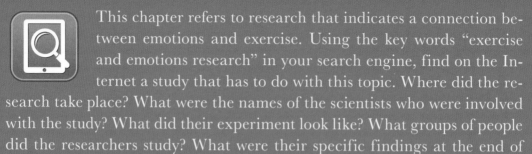
EXERCISE AND INTELLIGENCE

Neuroscientists used to think that the brain stopped making new nerve cells at birth. Whatever neurons you had when you were a newborn baby would be the most neurons you could possibly have for the rest of your life. Scientists also knew that some of the connections between neurons—the networks through which thoughts and memories travel—seemed to go away as a person got older. So based on all this, scientists were convinced that the number of neurons in a person's brain would become fewer with time. No new nerve cells would ever grow to take their place. But it turns out this isn't true!

Instead, *researchers* have discovered something amazing: in some people, even elderly people, new neurons are constantly being formed. The reason for this appears to have to do with how people interact with their environments—and exercise is a big part of that interaction.

One of the things that happen during exercise is increased blood flow throughout the entire body, including the brain. As more blood flows into the brain, more tiny blood vessels form—and these "micro blood vessels" appear to be connected to new neurons growing.

Text-Dependent Questions

1. According to this chapter, what causes emotions?
2. List four brain chemicals described in this chapter and explain how they're each connect to emotions.
3. What are three ways that exercise can improve your emotions?
4. Explain how exercise and intelligence may be connected.

Researchers still don't understand for sure how this process works or how it's connected to intelligence. But many experiments with both animals and people of all ages prove that there's a definite connection between exercise and brain cells.

So exercise! It's good for your brain.

Words to Understand

reflexes: Actions that your body performs automatically, without conscious thought.

diabetes: A disease where your body can't use sugar for energy correctly.

stimulates: Causes activity in a certain part of your body.

supple: Flexible and soft.

Chapter Three

EXERCISE
FOR YOUR FUTURE

Exercise is good for young adults. Once you start a regular exercise program, you'll notice you're feeling healthier and happier pretty quickly. But regular exercise now will also help you out years down the road. Exercise today—and your future self will thank you!

AGING AND THE BODY

As time goes by, the human body often doesn't work quite as well as it did when it was young. People may start to see a difference as early as twenty-five.

Our bodies change as we get older, and older people often can't do the same sort of activities that young people do. Exercising now, however, is the best way to make sure you're in shape later in life.

Exercise for Physical & Mental Health

Health often declines as we become older, but making healthy choices now is the best way to stay healthy in the future.

The heart is one of the places where this difference can be most obvious. A healthy twenty-five-year-old heart can pump at least 2.5 quarts of oxygen a minute when it's exercising (and athletes' hearts can pump even more), but a healthy sixty-five-year-old heart will pump less than 1.5 quarts of oxygen—and by the time that heart is eighty years old, it will only be pumping about a quart every minute. This means that less oxygen will be getting to the muscles and the rest of the body. And this is why older people get tired and out of breath more easily than younger people.

Exercising regularly when you're young is one of the best way to prevent many diseases and injuries that people face as they get older, including heart and muscular problems.

Exercise for Physical & Mental Health

At the same time that the heart is not working as well as it did when it was younger, the blood vessels are all getting stiffer, less elastic. This will make blood pressure climb as well, even when the person is sitting down doing nothing. High blood pressure all the time isn't good for the body. It can cause strokes and contribute to other diseases.

All this is bad enough, but the blood itself changes as a person gets older. It becomes thicker and stickier, which means the heart has to work harder just to pump the blood through the body. Meanwhile, the number of red blood cells—the cells that carry oxygen in the blood—goes down, so the blood doesn't carry as much oxygen to the body's cells.

Muscles change too as a person ages. Most people start to lose some of their muscles when they're in their forties, and that process will continue as they age. At the same time, muscles become tighter and less stretchy, as do the tendons and ligaments that connect muscles and bones. All this makes the muscles weaker. They can't do as much as they could when they were younger.

Changes are going on in the nervous system too. **Reflexes** are slower. Sleep may become more difficult, which can take a toll on mood, energy levels, and the immune system. As the connections between nerve cells in the brain break down, a person may no longer learn as easily. His memory may no longer be as good as it once was.

Now combine all that with the tendency that many people have to gain weight as they get older. If someone has fewer muscles and yet weighs more, just moving her body in simple ways becomes harder work. That can become a vicious circle—moving is hard, so the person exercises less, which makes her gain more weight, which in turn makes moving that much harder! Being overweight also contributes to more heart and blood pressure problems. It can lead to **diabetes** and other diseases.

All this sounds like really bad news, doesn't it? And you can't pretend the bad news just applies to your parents and other adults—because you too are going to experience all these things as you get older. No one can escape time!

EXERCISE AND AGING

You can't stop time—but when it comes to your body, you *can* slow down the effects time has on your body. And the way you do that is with exercise. Scientists have found that many of the changes we blame on age are actually caused by not using our bodies the way they are meant to be used.

Back in 1966, scientists first started to suspect the connections between exercise and feeling younger when researchers at the University of Texas Southwestern Medical School did a study on the effects of bed rest on the human body. Five healthy twenty-year-old men volunteered to spend three weeks doing nothing but lie in bed. At the beginning of the study, the researchers measured the men's heart rates, blood pressure, body fat, muscle strength, and the pumping capacity of their hearts—and then at the end of the three weeks, the researchers took all these measurements again. Here's what they found: after just three weeks, the bodies of those twenty-year-olds looked like the bodies of men twice their age!

The study didn't stop there, though. The researchers now put the same five men on an eight-week exercise program. At the end of the eight weeks, the bad effects of lying in bed for three weeks had totally

Make Connections

Researchers have found these connections between exercise and good health:

- Men who exercise regularly are 39 percent less likely to have heart attacks than men who don't exercise.
- People who exercise even at low levels reduce their chances of stroke by 24 percent—and regular moderate to strenuous exercise can reduce their chances of stroke by 46 percent.
- Exercise may even help fight cancer. Men who are very active are 47 percent less likely to get colon cancer.

disappeared. Many of the measurements were even better than they were before the men went on bed rest.

But that *still* wasn't the end of this research study. The five men in the experiment agreed to have scientists take a look at their bodies again thirty years later, when they were fifty years old. All five had stayed healthy; none of them had any serious diseases. Even so, the effects of time on their bodies were very clear. On average, they had each gained 50 pounds. Their percentages of body fat had increased, on average, from 14 percent to 28 percent. Their resting heart rates had increased, as had their blood pressure, while the pumping capacity of their hearts had dropped.

The researchers now put the volunteers back on an exercise program. This time, it was a gradual six-month plan that included walking, jogging, and cycling. And at the end of the six months? The men's resting heart rates, blood pressure, and the pumping ability of their hearts were right back to where they had been when the men were twenty years old, when they first entered the study!

Studies have found that exercise fights aging in other ways as well. Scientists at Harvard Medical School have found that exercise *stimulates* brain regions that are involved in memory to release a chemical

Text-Dependent Questions

1. Explain how an elderly person's heart is different from a young person's.
2. Besides changes to the heart, what are three other changes that take place in the body as a person ages?
3. What negative role does weight gain play in the aging process?
4. Describe the study that first proved the connection between aging and lack of exercise.
5. Using the sidebar on page 41, describe kinds of disease that exercise may help prevent.

that rewires these nerve circuits so they work better. This chemical isn't something you can get from a pill or a shot; only the brain can make it—and the brain *only* makes it when you exercise at least 30 minutes five times a week.

THE BEST KIND OF EXERCISE FOR YOUR FUTURE SELF

Researchers have found that endurance training is the best way to keep your heart, blood vessels, and lungs at their top performance. Endurance exercises help keep your muscles (including the muscles in your heart) *supple*. This kind of exercise also makes your blood vessel walls more elastic. It lowers your resting heart rate, and it makes your heart stronger so that it can deliver oxygen to all your body's organs and tissues.

Endurance exercise also burns calories—but even better, it keeps your metabolism from slowing down with age. This means you'll burn more calories even when you're resting, so you'll be less likely to gain weight.

Research Project

This chapter indicates that exercise could improve older people's memories. Use the Internet or the library to research connections between exercise and the prevention of dementia disorders such as Alzheimer's. What do you discover? Explain why or why not exercise can help fight dementia disorders. List research studies as evidence for your conclusions.

Endurance training also lifts your mood, improves sleep, and counteracts the effects of stress—and all this helps you better cope with life as you get older.

Everyone gets older. But being older doesn't need to mean being weaker and less healthy. Exercise can keep you strong for a lifetime.

And the best time to begin is right now.

Words to Understand

consistently: Being able to do something again and again without changing.

competition: When individuals try to beat each other to see who wins.

Chapter Four

MAKING A PLAN FOR PHYSICAL AND MENTAL HEALTH

Sometimes when people think about exercise programs, they focus on how being fit will make them *look*. They hope that exercise will give them the kind of bodies that models and athletes have. And of course, regular exercise *will* improve your muscle tone, and it can help you lose weight.

But what you look like really isn't as important as what you *feel* like. Regular exercise will make your body feel better, and it will make you feel better emotionally as well. Exercise will help you stay healthy and

Making an exercise plan may seem difficult at first, but it's a great way to make sure you exercise regularly and stay active. If you write down your goals, you'll have something to look back at so you don't forget.

Exercise for Physical & Mental Health

Sticking to your workout schedule is the most important part of making an exercise plan. Make sure your goals are realistic and that your schedule works for you.

happy through the years, as you become an adult and move through all the stages of your life ahead.

So it's important to create an exercise plan that's a good one for you, one that you'll be able to stick with for more than just a few weeks. You're not looking for short-terms benefits so much as a lifetime of good health!

Exercise falls into four basic categories: endurance, strength,

Finding exercises that are right for you will help you to stay on schedule and reach your fitness goals.

Exercise for Physical & Mental Health

balance, and flexibility. Different activities usually combine more than one category.

ENDURANCE

Endurance activities increase your breathing and heart rate. They keep your heart, lungs, and circulatory system healthy and improve your overall fitness. Here are some examples:

- brisk walking or walking uphill
- jogging
- yard work (mowing, raking, digging)
- dancing
- swimming
- cycling
- climbing stairs
- playing sports that involve a lot of running, like tennis, basketball, or hockey

STRENGTH

Strength exercises make your muscles stronger. These exercises are also called "strength training" or "resistance training." Examples include:

- weight lifting
- using a resistance band

BALANCE

These exercises are designed to improve your balance. Here are some examples:

- standing on one foot
- heel-to-toe walk
- tai chi

Playing sports is a great way to get active and stay fit. Whatever the activity that you love, get up and start participating.

Exercise for Physical & Mental Health

FLEXIBILITY

Flexibility exercises stretch your muscles, tendons, and ligaments. Being flexible gives you more freedom of movement for other exercises. Here are a couple of ways to do that:

- different kinds of stretches
- yoga

WHAT'S RIGHT FOR YOU?

Endurance exercise is the most important for overall good health, but you'll do best if you combine some of all four into your exercise plan. Your plan doesn't need to be very complicated, though. Your goal should simply be to **consistently** move your body several times a week—and move it enough that it makes your heart beat faster and your breath comes more quickly. Aside from that, it doesn't really matter what you do. If you pick something you enjoy doing, you'll be more likely to stick with it.

One thing that can help is if you link exercise with other activities you enjoy. If you're someone who enjoys **competition**, than sports might be your best bet for exercising. But if you're someone who enjoys being alone outdoors, then walking, jogging, or bicycling might be better choices for you. Do you enjoy doing things with a friend? Then walking or tennis could be good choices. Do you like meditation? Than you might consider getting involved with yoga or tai chi.

BE REALISTIC

Don't create an exercise plan for yourself that is too hard for you. Set yourself up for success by creating goals you can meet, rather than ones that are doomed for failure. You'll be more likely to stick with the plan if you don't get discouraged.

Once again, this means matching your exercise plan to your personality and your life. If you hate getting up early in the morning, for example, you're not likely to stick with an exercise plan that involves

If working out with a friend will keep you from missing that morning run or after school workout, find someone who feels the same and set a schedule to get fit together.

Exercise for Physical & Mental Health

Activities like yoga or aerobics can be done alone in your home, making them ideal workouts for people looking to get active by themselves.

jumping out of bed at 5 a.m. so you can go jogging before school—but you'll be more likely to stick with a plan to go for a walk every afternoon. If you hate to compete, then sports may not be the right form of exercise for you. If you're afraid of the water, don't build an exercise plan that focuses on swimming (even though you might want to tackle

Making a Plan for Physical and Mental Health   53

Starting small, with a walk or some light weights, is still starting. Getting off the couch and getting active is all that matters at first. Don't discourage yourself when you're starting to work out. You'll find that you'll be doing more than you thought you could in no time.

Exercise for Physical & Mental Health

Text-Dependent Questions

1. What role does motivation play in a successful exercise plan?
2. List five ways to make your exercise program "realistic," according to this chapter.
3. Explain how habit can be of help to your exercise program.
4. How does exercise have bearing on a person's future life?

your fear of water as a separate goal). Keep your family's schedule in mind as well; don't plan to spend evenings at the gym, for example, if you know your parents are relying on you to babysit regularly for your younger brother and sister.

If you haven't exercised for a while, don't start out by expecting yourself to be able to run 5 miles every day. Work up gradually to your exercise goals. Don't be afraid to start out small. For example, maybe at first you can work out for a half hour three times a week. After a while, push the length of your exercise session to 45 minutes—and then an hour. Try fitting in another exercise session every week. If you go gradually, you'll be more likely to enjoy your exercise and not get discouraged. You'll give your body time to get stronger. You'll start to feel the positive benefits of exercise. All that will help motivate you. Before long, you may find that you *want* to exercise five days a week for an hour at a time. Eventually, you may like it so much that you miss exercising if you skip a day!

Don't have an all-or-nothing attitude either. Say your exercise plan involves walking for an hour five days a week. But on Friday, you have to stay after school for language club, and then you and your friends are planning to go to a movie. It's going to be hard to fit an hour of walking into your busy day. But you might be able to fit in a half hour

Exercise is more than a way to stay in shape; it's a way of life. Getting active is one of the best ways to feel good about yourself and can help you in so many different ways. Starting today is the first step toward a better life!

Exercise for Physical & Mental Health

This book says in several places that exercise today has the power to change your future life. List five goals you have for your future. Then, using information contained in this book as well as additional research online or in the library, indicate how an exercise program could help you achieve these goals. Even if you don't think exercise has anything to do with your goals, dig deeper. You may be surprised by what you find!

during your lunch break—or even twenty minutes. A little is better than nothing!

Unless it helps you to stay motivated, don't compare yourself to others. Maybe your friends and you want to get some friendly competition going to see who can meet a particular fitness goal first. If that helps you, then it's fine. But fitness is a personal goal; it's about being the best *you* can be. You may never be a world-class athlete, but that's okay! Your goal is to be as physically fit as you can be.

STICK WITH IT!

The important thing is to not give up. If one kind of exercise doesn't seem right for you, feel free to switch to something else. Try out a bunch of different forms of exercise to see which one you enjoy most. Whatever you do, make it fun!

Eventually, if you stick with exercising, it will become a habit. Habits are behaviors we do automatically, without giving them much thought. For example, once taking a shower every day becomes a habit, you don't get up in the morning and debate with yourself whether or not you should shower. You just jump in the shower. You may even do it on autopilot, barely realizing what you're doing.

Even on your busiest days, you'll probably still find time to fit in the fifteen minutes it takes to shower. When exercise becomes a habit in the same way, it will be just a normal part of your day. You'll be less likely to find excuses to skip it.

And the more you exercise, the healthier you will be. Your heart, lungs, brain, and all the rest of your body's organs will be working at their top potential. You'll feel happier and calmer. You might even be a little smarter—and you could live longer. Isn't all that worth it?

FIND OUT MORE

In Books

American College of Sports Medicine. *ACSM's Complete Guide to Fitness & Health*. Champion, Ill.: Human Kinetics, 2012.

Bounds, Laura, Kirsten Brekken Shea, Dottiedee Agnor, and Gayden Darnell. *Health & Fitness: A Guide to a Healthy Lifestyle*. Dubuque, Iowa: Kendall Hunt, 2012.

Greenfield, Ben. *Beyond Training: Mastering Endurance, Health, and Life*. Las Vegas, Nev.: Victory Belt Publishing, 2014.

Maffetone, Philip. *The Big Book of Health and Fitness*. New York: Skyhorse, 2012.

Sharkey, Brian and Steven Gaskill. *Fitness & Health*. Champion, Ill.: Human Kinetics, 2013.

Online

The Benefits of Physical Activity
www.hsph.harvard.edu/nutritionsource/staying-active-full-story

Exercise and Your Emotions
healthyliving.azcentral.com/exercise-emotionally-4592.html

Seven Benefits of Regular Physical Activity
www.mayoclinic.org/exercise/art-20048389

Train Your Brain: Can Jogging Make You Smarter?
www.independent.co.uk/life-style/health-and-families/healthy-living/train-your-brain-can-jogging-make-you-smarter-800168.html

The Unexpected Benefits of Exercise
greatist.com/fitness/13-awesome-mental-health-benefits-exercise

SERIES GLOSSARY OF KEY TERMS

abs: Short for abdominals. The muscles in the middle of your body, located over your stomach and intestines.

aerobic: A process by which energy is steadily released using oxygen. Aerobic exercise focuses on breathing and exercising for a long time.

anaerobic: When lots of energy is quickly released, without using oxygen. You can't do anaerobic exercises for a very long time.

balance: Your ability to stay steady and upright.

basal metabolic rate: How many calories your body burns naturally just by breathing and carrying out other body processes.

bodybuilding: Exercising specifically to get bigger, stronger muscles.

calories: The units of energy that your body uses. You get calories from food and you use them up when you exercise.

carbohydrates: The foods that your body gets most of its energy from. Common foods high in carbohydrates include sugars and grains.

cardiovascular system: Your heart and blood vessels.

circuit training: Rapidly switching from one exercise to another in a cycle. Circuit training helps build endurance in many different muscle groups.

circulatory system: The system of blood vessels in your body, which brings oxygen and nutrients to your cells and carries waste products away.

cool down: A gentle exercise that helps your body start to relax after a workout.

core: The muscles of your torso, including your abs and back muscles.

cross training: When an athlete trains for a sport she normally doesn't play, to exercise any muscle groups she might be weak in.

dehydration: When you don't have enough water in your body. When you exercise, you lose water by sweating, and it's important to replace it.

deltoids: The thick muscles covering your shoulder joint.

energy: The power your body needs to do things like move around and keep you alive.

endurance: The ability to keep going for a long time.

flexibility: How far you can bend, or how far your muscles can stretch.

glutes: Short for gluteals, the muscles in your buttocks.

hydration: Taking in more water to keep from getting dehydrated.

isometric: An exercise that you do without moving, by holding one position.

isotonic: An exercise you do by moving your muscles.

lactic acid: A chemical that builds up in your muscles after you exercise. It causes a burning feeling during anaerobic exercises.

lats: Short for latissimus dorsi, the large muscles along your back.

metabolism: How fast you digest food and burn energy.

muscle: The parts of your body that contract and expand to allow you to move.

nervous system: Made up of your brain, spinal cord, and nerves, which carry messages between your brain, spinal cord, and the rest of your body.

nutrition: The chemical parts of the food you eat that your body needs to survive and use energy.

obliques: The muscles to either side of your stomach, under your ribcage.

pecs: Short for pectorals, the muscles on your chest.

quads: Short for quadriceps, the large muscle on the front of your upper leg and thigh.

reps: How many times you repeat an anaerobic exercise in a row.

strength: The power of your muscles.

stretching: Pulling on your muscles to make them longer. Stretching before you exercise can keep you flexible and prevent injuries.

warm up: A light exercise you do before a workout to get your body ready for harder exercise.

weight training: Exercises that involve lifting heavy weights to increase your strength and endurance.

INDEX

adrenaline 29, 31
aging 35, 39–42
alveoli 22
anxiety 26, 29–30
ATP 13, 15, 24

bicycling 12, 51
blood 8, 11, 13, 15, 17, 19,
    21–25, 32, 39–42
blood pressure 19, 21–22, 39–
    41
blood vessels 8, 15, 17, 19,
    22–23, 25, 32, 39, 42
bone 13, 39
brain 8, 14, 23, 25–27, 29–33,
    39, 41–42, 58

calories 24–25, 42
carbon dioxide 15, 21, 24
cells 8–9, 11, 13, 19, 21, 23–25,
    29, 32–33, 39
circulatory system 17, 19, 21, 49

dancing 49
depression 29
diabetes 34, 39
diaphragm 22
digestion 22
dopamine 29

emotion 29, 32–33
endorphins 29, 31
endurance training 40, 42–43
energy 13, 21, 24–25, 34, 39
evaporation 21
exercise program (plan) 11–13,
    35, 40–41, 45, 55, 57

fat 24–25, 40–41
flexibility 47, 49

glucose 21, 24

heart 11–13, 15, 17, 19, 21, 29,
    37–42, 49, 51, 58
heat 15, 21–23
hemoglobin 21, 25
hypothalamus 23

intestine 9, 24

jogging 12, 40–41, 49, 51

lactic acid 15
liver 24
lungs 9, 11–12, 15, 17, 19–22,
    29, 40, 42, 49, 58

memory 39, 41
metabolism 24–25, 42

motivation 8–9, 55
muscle 11–15, 17, 19–25, 37,
    39–40, 42, 45, 49

nervous system 14–15, 17, 21,
    25–27, 39
neuron 29, 32

oxygen 11–12, 15, 17, 19–22,
    25, 30, 37, 39–40, 42

pain 12, 29

red blood cell 21, 39
research 24, 32, 41, 43, 57
running 25, 40, 49

serotonin 29
skin 17, 22–23, 25
sports 2, 21, 28, 49–51, 53
sports drinks 21
strength 40, 47, 49
stress 30–31, 43
stroke 8, 19, 21, 41
sweat 21, 23
swimming 12, 40, 49, 53

tai chi 49, 51
tissue 8, 12–13, 15, 42

waste 15, 21
weight lifting 12, 49

yoga 51, 53

ABOUT THE AUTHOR AND THE CONSULTANT

Z.B. Hill is an author and publicist living in Binghamton, NY. He has written books on a variety of topics including mental health, music, and fitness.

Diane H. Hart, Nationally Certified Fitness Professional and Health Specialist, has designed and implemented fitness and wellness programs for more than twenty years. She is a master member of the International Association of Fitness Professionals, and a health specialist for Blue Shield of Northeastern New York, HealthNow, and Palladian Health. In 2010, Diane was elected president of the National Association for Health and Fitness (NAHF), a nonprofit organization that exists to improve the quality of life for individuals in the United States through the promotion of physical fitness, sports, and healthy lifestyles. NAHF accomplishes this work by fostering and supporting state governors and state councils and coalitions that promote and encourage regular physical activity. NAHF is also the national sponsor of Employee Health and Fitness Month, the largest global workplace health and fitness event each May. American College of Sports Medicine (ACSM) has been a strategic partner with NAHF since 2009.

PICTURE CREDITS